Love Is God

5¢

written by Marie Frost
illustrated by Heidi Petach

2969 ✓

©1986, The STANDARD PUBLISHING Company, Cincinnati, Ohio
Division of STANDEX INTERNATIONAL Corporation. Printed in Italy.

Love is Mother,
    Who listens to me
When I am troubled,
    And when I'm happy.

Can you find Mother?
What do you think Billy is telling his
   mother?
Do you talk to your mother?

Love is Father,
    Who helps me see
God will always
    Care for me.

Point to Father.
What is he doing to help Sandy feel less
  afraid?
Does God take care of you when it storms?

Love is Grandfather,
Who lets me talk
When we are going
For a walk.

Are Grandfather and Sally in a hurry?
Do you think they stop to smell the
    flowers?
Why is everyone else in a hurry?

Love is Grandmother,
  Who mixes gingerbread,
And turns it into
  A man instead.

Point to Grandmother.
What are Penny and Sam doing to help?
What does your grandmother bake that is
   special?

Love is Sister,
   Who reads storybooks,
And always gives me
   Time to look.

Can you find Sister reading to Mindy?
Do you like someone to read to you?
What is your favorite story?

Love is Brother,
   Who sees my toes,
And sprinkles them clean
   With a garden hose.

Point to big Brother.
Does Ted look like he is enjoying himself?
How does it feel to have your toes
    sprinkled with the hose?

Love is a friend,
 Who comes to play
When I am lonely,
 On a rainy day.

Can you find Jerry and his friend?
What games do you think Jerry and his
    friend will play?
Do you have a good friend who plays with
    you?

Love is Sunday school,
Where I like to be.
My teacher is always
Glad to see me.

Point to David's Sunday-school teacher.
What do you think she is saying to David?
Do you listen to your teacher?

Love is God,
   And I love Him too.
I can tell Him,
   "I love You!"

Point to Mark. What is he doing?
Do you tell God, "I love You"?
What else do you say to God when you
   pray?

Have someone help you sing this song about love

I Am Happy

M.H.F.

Marie H. Frost

I am hap-py, hap-py, hap-py, I'm as hap-py as can be, I am glad that I love *God,— And I know that *God loves me.—

* Mother/she; Father/he; Sister/she; Brother/he.